TEZOS: THE KINGDOM OF ART

Luca Filigheddu

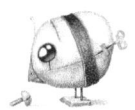

This book is dedicated to my wife, my kids and my dog.

*A special dedication to my father, who
passed away on Jan 18, 2024.*

CONTENTS

Tezos: The Kingdom of Art

Luca Filigheddu aka Filos.tez

"Tezos: The Kingdom of Art" invites artists on an exhilarating journey into the dynamic dimension where creativity meets technology. In this illuminating guide, the author shares a treasure trove of insights, tips, and strategies to help artists embark on a new business venture by harnessing the transformative power of blockchain technology. Dive into a world where Tezos reigns as the gateway to infinite artistic possibilities, where NFTs become the digital keys to your kingdom of art. Discover the secrets to minting, marketing, and monetizing your creations while navigating the decentralized landscape with confidence. Whether you're a seasoned artist or just beginning your creative odyssey, this book unveils the keys to unlocking success in the vibrant kingdom of Tezos, where innovation knows no bounds, and artists rule the digital realm.

Cover: Toy Bird by Fer Sassali - Handmade, pencil

WHY WE ARE HERE

Hi, my name is Luca and I'm better known as "@filos" on X.

My journey in the complex and fascinating world made of "blockchains" and "NFTs" started in January 2021.

I don't know if you, dear reader, already know what I'm talking about, but I'm sure you'll learn more by reading this book until the end.

During this period, I bought and sold hundreds of NFTs and digital artworks and at the time of writing this book I own a collection of almost 500 artworks by hundreds of artists from different parts of the world. It's not a huge collection, there are collectors who own tens of thousands, but considering I accumulated 300+ only in the past two months, I consider it a quickly growing collection.

That being said, my goal with this book is to provide you, artists around the world, with an easy-to-understand manual on how to sell your art online, making sure the intellectual property is protected and your art can easily be recognised as your art, and yours only.

If you want to start selling your beautiful artwork online, please keep reading this book. For any questions, don't hesitate to contact me on X, I'm always available.

My profile on X: https://twitter.com/filos

1. SELLING YOUR ART ONLINE

Artwork, as defined by the "Britannica" encyclopaedia, encompasses various creative forms like paintings, sculptures, and photographs, serving the purpose of conveying beauty or significant ideas and emotions. Throughout history, human expression has taken shape through diverse mediums, from traditional pen and paper to the rudimentary chiseling of stone and the revolutionary invention of the camera in the late 1800s. These inventive methods have allowed individuals to share their inner worlds and external experiences, leaving a tangible mark on our cultural heritage.

However, the advent of the digital age and the proliferation of online platforms have ushered in a new artistic creation and dissemination era. In the physical world, establishing the origin of an artwork is usually straightforward, even though the act of copying remains a common practice within the art world. Online, this narrative transforms into something quite distinct.

Imagine, for a moment, capturing a photograph of your meticulously crafted painting or a breathtaking piece of scenery during your travels, either as a hobbyist or a professional photographer. You eagerly share your creation online, only for it to be effortlessly snatched and posted elsewhere without any attribution to the artist behind the lens or brushstroke. Regrettably, this scenario can perpetuate as others replicate, modify, and re-share your work, each step further obfuscating the true source of the original masterpiece.

This predicament extends to all digital creations, whether they're born on a tablet screen using innovative painting tools or captured as captivating moments through the lens of a camera. While one can passionately declare, "I took it, I made it, I created it," the glaring absence of a tangible way to substantiate these claims poses a formidable challenge in the realm of selling digital artwork online. Placing your digital treasures in an online store, though a viable option, opens the door to potential intellectual property theft as unscrupulous individuals copy and resell your creations under their own authorship.

However, hope emerges from the technological horizon with the groundbreaking advent of blockchain technology. This innovation introduces a transformative solution to the age-old problem of authenticating the origin and ownership of digital art. Through blockchain, artists can now firmly establish their creative precedence and assert their intellectual property rights with unprecedented transparency and security. This groundbreaking technology not only safeguards the fruits of an artist's labor but also paves the way for a new era in which creators can confidently share their digital masterpieces with the world, secure in the knowledge that their artistic legacy remains unassailable.

2. INTELLECTUAL PROPERTY

T he issue of intellectual property in the digital age is a complex and pervasive one. The phrase, "Hey, I made it, not you. Why are you selling my photo online without my permission?" encapsulates the frustration felt by countless artists who have seen their digital creations misappropriated and exploited without consent.

This phenomenon is not a recent development; it has plagued artists ever since the advent of computers and the migration of artistic expression to the online realm. The digital age brought with it unprecedented opportunities for artists to showcase their talents and monetise their work, but it also brought about a formidable challenge: how to protect their intellectual property in a virtual world where copies can be easily reproduced and disseminated.

In the physical world, the art of detecting fakes and forgeries has been honed over centuries. From scrutinizing brushwork to analyzing chemical compositions, experts have developed methods to distinguish genuine artworks from replicas. This applies not only to art but also to other sectors like fashion and horology, where counterfeits abound. Over time, through the establishment of provenance records, the use of watermarks, and advancements in forensic analysis, people have become adept at discerning genuine articles from imitations.

However, in the digital world, the landscape changes dramatically. When an artist creates a masterpiece on their iPad and shares it online, the very act of dissemination can cast doubt on their authorship in the future. The ease with which digital assets can be copied and shared exponentially increases the risk of unauthorised duplication, making it challenging to establish a definitive record of ownership.

For artists, this quandary has posed significant limitations on their ability to leverage the vast potential of the internet to showcase their creations and generate income. The desire to ensure that the credit and benefits rightfully go to the creators themselves has been a central concern.

Enter Non-Fungible Tokens (NFTs), a revolutionary solution that has emerged to address this challenge. NFTs, powered by blockchain technology, offer artists a means to authenticate and assert their authorship over digital assets with unmatched clarity and security. Each NFT is a unique token that links a specific digital creation to its creator through a transparent and immutable blockchain record. This innovation not only safeguards the intellectual property of artists but also provides collectors and buyers with irrefutable proof of ownership and authenticity.

In essence, NFTs serve as a digital certificate of authenticity, revolutionising the way artists share and sell their work online. They empower creators to confidently bring their art to the digital world, knowing that the trail of their authorship remains unassailable, ushering in a new era where artists can truly enjoy the fruits of their digital labor.

3. WHAT IS AN NFT?

An NFT, or Non-Fungible Token, is a type of digital asset that represents ownership or proof of authenticity of a unique item or piece of content using blockchain technology. Unlike cryptocurrencies such as Bitcoin or Ethereum (ever heard about them?), which are fungible and can be exchanged on a one-to-one basis (1 Bitcoin is always equal to 1 Bitcoin), NFTs are non-fungible, meaning each one is distinct and cannot be exchanged on a like-for-like basis with another NFT.

As you can easily understand, this is exactly the technical solution that can be used to solve the issue mentioned in the previous paragraph.

Key characteristics of NFTs include:

• Uniqueness: Each NFT has a distinct digital signature, making it one-of-a-kind or part of a limited edition.
• Indivisibility: NFTs cannot be divided into smaller units like cryptocurrencies. You either own the whole NFT or none of it.
• Ownership and Provenance: NFTs are recorded on a blockchain, providing a transparent and immutable ledger of ownership and transaction history. This ensures that the owner of an NFT can prove its authenticity and origin.

Let me repeat: NFTs ensure that the owner can prove its authenticity and origin. So if an artist creates something and wants to make sure everyone knows he/she is the author and/or the owner, NFTs come in to help. They just have to create (mint) a new NFT representing their artwork.

This is the reason why artists, musicians, game developers, and content creators can tokenize their work as NFTs and sell them in online marketplaces. Buyers of NFTs receive a digital certificate of ownership and the ability to transfer or resell the NFT.

Creating an NFT is very easy and we will cover it in the next paragraph. It's very important to highlight that you don't need any technical expertise to do that because the tech complexity is hidden behind other easy tools everyone can use.

4. TEZOS, THE PLACE TO BE

In the previous paragraph, I mentioned two important keywords that are crucial in order to allow artists to sell their artworks online: NFT and blockchain.

The definition of NFT was described in the previous paragraph, but what about the concept of blockchain?

First of all, let me make it clear: you, as an artist, just need to know that it is a technology that exists and it's your best friend when it comes to selling your art online. No need to have a deep understanding of how it works, so I will just quickly describe what blockchains are.

A blockchain is a decentralized and distributed digital ledger technology that records transactions across multiple computers in a way that ensures the integrity, transparency, and security of the data. It was originally developed as the underlying technology for the cryptocurrency Bitcoin, but its applications have since expanded beyond digital currencies to a wide range of industries.

Key characteristics and concepts of a blockchain include:

1. *Decentralization:* Instead of relying on a central authority like a bank or government, blockchain operates on a network of computers (nodes) that collectively maintain the ledger. This decentralization helps prevent a single point of failure and reduces the risk of manipulation.

2. *Transparency*: All transactions recorded on a blockchain are visible to all participants in the network. This transparency ensures that everyone can verify the authenticity of transactions.

3. *Security*: Blockchains use cryptographic techniques to secure data and transactions. Each block (a group of transactions) is linked to the previous one through a cryptographic hash, creating a chain. Changing the data in one block would require changing all subsequent blocks, making it extremely difficult and computationally expensive to tamper with the ledger.

4. *Immutability*: Once a transaction is recorded on the blockchain, it is nearly impossible to alter or delete it. This immutability is a core feature of blockchains and adds to their trustworthiness.

5. *Consensus Mechanisms:* Blockchains use consensus algorithms to ensure that all participants agree on the state of the ledger. Common consensus mechanisms include Proof of Work (PoW) and Proof of Stake (PoS).

6. *Smart Contracts:* Some blockchains, like Ethereum, support smart contracts. These are self-executing contracts with predefined rules and conditions. They automate processes and transactions when specific conditions are met.

7. *Public and Private Blockchains:* Blockchains can be public (open to anyone) or private (restricted to specific participants or organizations). Public blockchains, like Bitcoin, Ethereum and Tezos, are accessible to anyone, while private blockchains are typically used within organisations or consortia for specific purposes.

Blockchains have a wide range of applications, including:

- Cryptocurrencies: The most well-known use case, where cryptocurrencies like Bitcoin and Ethereum use blockchain technology to record and verify transactions.
- Supply Chain Management: Tracking the movement of goods, verifying the authenticity of products, and ensuring transparency in the supply chain.
- Finance and Banking: Streamlining financial transactions, improving cross-border payments, and reducing fraud.

- Healthcare: Securing and sharing patient data, ensuring the integrity of medical records, and tracking the pharmaceutical supply chain.
- Voting Systems: Creating transparent and secure electronic voting systems.
- Real Estate: Simplifying property transactions and land registry management.
- Identity Verification: Providing secure and decentralized identity verification solutions.

But the application that we care about the most here is the ability to create and sell NFTs representing an artwork, your artwork.

Overall, blockchain technology has the potential to disrupt various industries by providing a trustless and efficient way to record and verify data and transactions. This is what is happening in art. You can create NFTs representing your creations and trade them on certain blockchains, that will do their job tracking the transactions and making sure all happens in a transparent and verifiable way.

While in theory, you could publish your artwork on any blockchain, there are many different reasons why I highly recommend any artist out there to publish and trade their art on Tezos.

Tezos blockchain offers several advantages for artists, compared to other blockchains like Ethereum. Its energy-efficient proof-of-stake consensus mechanism aligns with environmental concerns, and low transaction fees make it cost-effective for artists to mint and sell NFTs. Tezos provides customizable smart contracts, allowing artists to create unique mechanisms for engaging with their audience and managing royalties. The Tezos community is supportive of digital art, with emerging NFT marketplaces and platforms. Not only that, the community is incredibly strong and responsive and the main driver is not speculation or "making quick money", but it's rather spreading the word about art and beauty.

The blockchain's scalability, security, and governance participation options provide confidence to artists, while interoperability opens up opportunities for cross-chain interactions. Let's see all these points more in detail in the next chapter.

5. THE TEZOS BLOCKCHAIN

Whether you are an artist who has always published on the Ethereum blockchain (until now) or just an artist trying to sell their first artwork online, there are several very good reasons why you should start publishing ("minting") and selling your artwork on the Tezos blockchain.

First of all, taking into account the description of "blockchain" given above, let me give you some additional information on the Tezos blockchain and how it is different from Ethereum.

ALERT: 99.9% of the information contained in the following paragraph could be irrelevant to you, the artist. There could be artists who want to get more technical information because are curious, others, instead, who don't care at all. If you are not interested, feel free to jump straight to Chapter 6.

The Tezos blockchain was invented by Arthur Breitman and Kathleen Breitman. They are a husband-and-wife team who co-founded the project. The development of Tezos began in 2014 when the white-paper was published, and it was officially launched in June 2018.

Arthur Breitman has a background in mathematics, computer science, and finance. Originally from France, he studied mathematics at the École Polytechnique and then pursued further studies at the Courant Institute of Mathematical Sciences at New York University.

Before co-founding Tezos, Arthur worked in various roles, including as a quantitative analyst at Goldman Sachs and a quantitative researcher at the asset management firm DE Shaw.

His technical expertise and deep understanding of mathematics and finance played a significant role in the development of Tezos.

On the other hand, Kathleen Breitman has a background in business and operations. She studied at Cornell University, where she earned a degree in history and cognitive science. Prior to her involvement in blockchain, Kathleen worked at companies like R3, Accenture, and Bridgewater Associates, gaining experience in different areas, including consulting and finance.

Kathleen's business acumen and experience in finance and technology complement Arthur's technical expertise.

Together, they conceived the idea of a self-amending blockchain with on-chain governance, which became one of the defining features of Tezos.

The Tezos project gained attention for its innovative approach to blockchain governance and its focus on security and formal verification. It raised significant funds during its initial coin offering in 2017 (an initial coin offering - ICO - is the cryptocurrency industry's equivalent of an initial public offering - IPO -...a company seeking to raise money to create a new coin, app, or service can launch an ICO as a way to raise funds), making it one of the largest ICOs at the time, totaling approximately 66,000 BTC (Bitcoin) and 361,000 ETH (Ethereum). This amount was equivalent to hundreds of millions of US dollars.

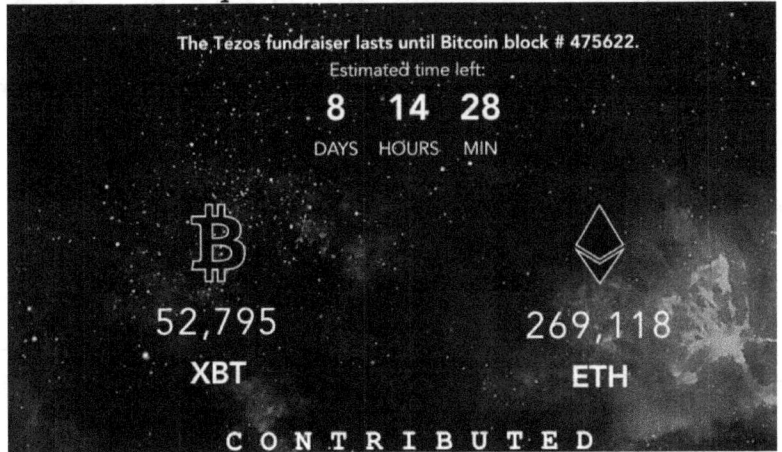

The Tezos fundraiser lasts until Bitcoin block # 475622.
Estimated time left:

8   14   28
DAYS HOURS MIN

52,795
XBT

269,118
ETH

CONTRIBUTED

Since its launch, Tezos has continued to develop its technology and ecosystem, attracting developers and projects to build on its blockchain.

Tezos is a blockchain platform that is designed to be self-amending, decentralized, and highly secure. It was created to address some of the challenges and limitations found in earlier blockchain technologies, such as Ethereum and Bitcoin. Here are some key features and aspects of the Tezos blockchain:

1. *Self-Amendment:* One of the defining features of Tezos is its ability to upgrade itself through a process known as on-chain governance. Tezos stakeholders can propose and vote on protocol upgrades, enabling the blockchain to evolve over time without the need for contentious hard forks. This self-amendment mechanism is intended to make the Tezos network more adaptable and resistant to contentious development disputes.

2. *Smart Contracts:* Tezos supports smart contracts, which are self-executing contracts with predefined rules and conditions (as we mentioned in the previous paragraph). Developers can use the Tezos blockchain to create decentralized applications (DApps) and automate various processes. This is no different from other blockchains like Ethereum for example.

3. *Delegated Proof of Stake (DPoS):* Tezos uses a consensus mechanism known as Delegated Proof of Stake, which involves token holders delegating their coins to validators (known as "bakers" in Tezos). Validators are responsible for creating new blocks and validating transactions. DPoS is chosen to increase scalability and energy efficiency.

4. *Formal Verification:* Tezos places a strong emphasis on security and correctness. It supports formal verification, which is a mathematical method for ensuring that smart contracts behave as intended and are free from vulnerabilities.

5. *Liquid Proof of Stake:* Tezos incorporates a concept called "liquid proof of stake," which means that token holders can actively participate in governance and receive rewards for doing

so.

6. *Decentralization:* Tezos aims to be a decentralized blockchain network, with its governance and consensus mechanisms designed to avoid centralization. Validators are regularly rotated, and token holders play an active role in decision-making.

7. *Interoperability:* Tezos has the potential to interact with other blockchain networks and financial systems through its ability to adapt and upgrade its protocols. This can enable cross-chain compatibility and interactions with various decentralized finance (DeFi) platforms.

8. *Token (XTZ):* XTZ ꜩ is the native cryptocurrency of the Tezos network. It is used for transaction fees, staking, and participating in governance decisions.

All that said, how is Tezos different from the well-known (sometimes better-known) Ethereum blockchain?

Tezos and Ethereum are both blockchain platforms designed for decentralized applications (DApps) and smart contracts, but they differ in several key ways:

1. *Governance and Upgrades:*

- Tezos: Tezos has a built-in mechanism for on-chain governance, allowing token holders to propose and vote on protocol upgrades. This self-amendment process is intended to make the network more adaptable and prevent contentious hard forks.

- Ethereum: Ethereum has historically relied on hard forks to implement significant upgrades. While Ethereum 2.0 is working on a transition to a more scalable and secure platform, the upgrade process is different from Tezos, and it has faced challenges and debates.

2. *Consensus Mechanism:*

- Tezos: Tezos uses a Delegated Proof of Stake (DPoS) variant, where token holders can delegate their coins to validators (bakers). DPoS is chosen to increase scalability and energy efficiency.

- Ethereum: Ethereum currently uses a Proof of Stake (PoS) mechanism for its Ethereum 2.0 upgrade, which aims to improve scalability and energy efficiency. Previously, it used a Proof of Work (PoW) mechanism like Bitcoin.

3. *Programming Language:*

- Tezos: Tezos offers a unique smart contract language called Michelson, which is designed for formal verification and security. Developers can also use LIGO and other higher-level languages.

- Ethereum: Ethereum primarily uses Solidity for smart contract development, and it introduced Vyper as a more secure and readable alternative. Ethereum developers have more language options and a larger developer community.

4. *Formal Verification:*

- Tezos: Tezos places a strong emphasis on formal verification, a method for mathematically proving the correctness and security of smart contracts.

- Ethereum: While Ethereum supports formal verification, it is not as deeply integrated as in Tezos.

5. *Staking and Governance Participation:*

- Tezos: Tezos token holders can participate in governance decisions and earn rewards by staking their tokens.

- Ethereum: Ethereum is transitioning to a PoS mechanism that allows token holders to stake and participate in network security. Ethereum's governance model is evolving as well.

6. *Native Tokens:*

- Tezos: The native cryptocurrency of Tezos is called XTZ (Tezzies), used for transaction fees, staking, and governance participation.

- Ethereum: Ethereum's native cryptocurrency is ETH, serving similar purposes as XTZ.

7. *Interoperability:*

- Tezos: Tezos aims to provide interoperability with other blockchains and financial systems through its adaptability and upgradability.

- Ethereum: Ethereum has numerous bridge projects and protocols aimed at achieving interoperability with other blockchains.

8. *Adaptive and Self-Upgrade:*

- Tezos: Tezos can adapt and upgrade itself without contentious hard forks, which may help prevent community splits.

- Ethereum: Ethereum's history includes contentious hard forks, such as the Ethereum vs. Ethereum Classic split.

It's important to note that both Tezos and Ethereum have their own strengths and weaknesses, and their suitability for specific use cases may depend on factors such as security requirements, governance preferences, and developer familiarity with the platform.

6. PUBLISHING YOUR ARTWORK

I n the preceding chapter, I emphasised the importance of acquiring fundamental knowledge about the technologies essential for your future endeavors on Tezos. Now, it's time to roll up your sleeves and dive into the process of publishing and selling your artwork on the Tezos blockchain.

Your first crucial step, even before anything else, is to create a new wallet specifically tailored for Tezos. This wallet serves as the secure repository where you'll not only safeguard your funds in the form of XTZ cryptocurrency but also store your valuable artwork in the form of NFTs. As you successfully sell your NFTs, the funds collected from buyers will flow into this dedicated wallet. Importantly, this wallet will also facilitate your ability to cover the exceptionally low fees associated with any actions you undertake on the Tezos blockchain.

There are several wallets available and I don't want to force you to use one or another, but all the examples I will make in this book will make use of the **Kukai Wallet**.

For your reference, in case you prefer using another wallet, here is a list of ten wallets you can use on Tezos.

1. *Galleon Wallet:* Galleon is an open-source wallet designed specifically for Tezos. It offers a user-friendly interface and features like delegation and baking support. A mobile app for iOS and Android is available, too. The latest updates on their X account are from August 2023, but the Android app has not been updated since 2021, so

I'm not sure this wallet is currently under development or not.

2. *Temple Wallet:* Temple Wallet, tailored for the Tezos blockchain, is a well-known mobile wallet and browser extension. It offers user-friendly access to Tezos (XTZ) tokens and decentralized applications (dApps) on the Tezos platform. You can conveniently use Temple Wallet as a browser extension with popular web browsers to engage with Tezos dApps and handle your XTZ tokens and NFTs. Mobile apps for iOS and Android are available, too.

3. *Atomic Wallet:* Atomic Wallet is a multi-currency wallet that supports Tezos along with a wide range of other cryptocurrencies. It provides a desktop and mobile app version for easy access.

4. *Trust Wallet:* Trust Wallet is a mobile wallet that supports Tezos and various other cryptocurrencies. It's known for its user-friendly interface and security features.

5. *Kukai Wallet:* Kukai is a web-based wallet designed for Tezos. It is a non-custodial wallet, which means you have full control over your private keys.

6. *Ledger Nano S/X:* If you're looking for a hardware wallet for Tezos, both the Ledger Nano S and Ledger Nano X support XTZ. Hardware wallets are considered one of the most secure options for storing cryptocurrencies.

7. *Trezor Model T:* Trezor Model T is another hardware wallet option that supports Tezos. It offers a secure and user-friendly way to store your XTZ.

8. *Exodus Wallet:* Exodus is a multi-currency desktop wallet that supports Tezos along with many other cryptocurrencies. It provides a visually appealing interface and exchange functionality.

9. *ZenGo Wallet:* Zengo Wallet is a cryptocurrency wallet

designed to provide a secure and user-friendly way to manage various digital assets. Zengo Wallet is known for its innovative approach to wallet security and recovery. Zengo Wallet does not rely on traditional private keys for security. Instead, it uses a combination of cutting-edge technology, such as threshold signatures, to ensure that your wallet remains secure without the need for complicated private key management. ZenGo is available as a mobile app for iOS and Android.

10. *AirGap Wallet:* AirGap is a mobile wallet with a unique approach to security. It offers a two-device setup, with one device used for wallet management and another for signing transactions, enhancing security.

Creating a wallet with Kukai

Creating a Tezos wallet with Kukai is a straightforward process. Kukai is a web-based wallet for Tezos that allows you to manage your XTZ and interact with the Tezos blockchain.

It's the wallet I use regularly and it works incredibly well. It's web-based, so can be easily used from any browser on any platform.

Here are the steps to create a Tezos wallet using Kukai:

1. Visit the Kukai Wallet Website:

Open your web browser and go to the Kukai wallet website: https://kukai.app/.

2. Create a New Wallet:

On the Kukai homepage, click on the "Create a Wallet" button. This will start the process of creating a new Tezos wallet.

3. Set a Strong Password:

Choose a strong and secure password for your wallet. Make sure it's something that you can remember, as you'll need it to access your wallet in the future. Confirm the password.

4. Download and Store Your Seed Phrase:

Kukai will generate a 24-word seed phrase for your wallet. This seed phrase is crucial for recovering your wallet if you ever lose access to it. Download

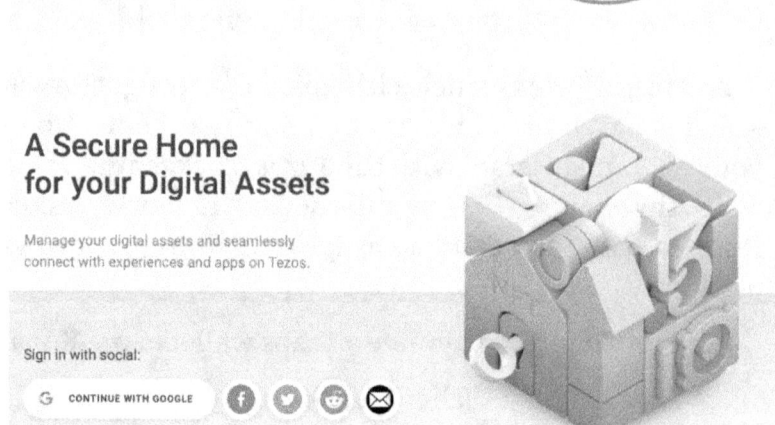

the seed phrase and store it securely offline. Do not share it with anyone and keep it in a safe place.

5. Confirm Your Seed Phrase:

To ensure you've saved your seed phrase correctly, Kukai will ask you to confirm it. Re-enter the 24 words in the correct order.

6. Wallet Created:

Once you've successfully confirmed your seed phrase, your Tezos wallet will be created. You can now access and manage your wallet.

7. Access Your Wallet:

To access your wallet in the future, simply visit the Kukai wallet website and click on "Access Wallet." Enter your password and seed phrase to log in.

8. Receive and Send XTZ:

With your Kukai wallet, you can receive XTZ by sharing your wallet address with others. You can also send XTZ to other Tezos addresses using the wallet's functionality.

9. Delegate (Optional):

If you want to participate in Tezos' proof-of-stake consensus mechanism and earn rewards by staking your XTZ, you can delegate your tokens using Kukai. Look for the delegation section in the wallet's interface.

Remember to keep your password and seed phrase secure and never share them with anyone. Losing your seed phrase means losing access to your funds. Additionally, be cautious of phishing sites and only use the official Kukai website to access your wallet.

Minting your artwork

objkt.com

The largest Digital Art & Collectible marketplace on Tezos

Buy and sell your NFTs on our marketplace or try out an English or a Dutch Auction.

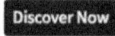

Now that you have your wallet up and running, the next step is selling your artwork through an online marketplace.

There are various marketplaces, but over the years objkt.com has become the most popular marketplace where artists sell and buy artworks on Tezos.

Selling an artwork on Objkt is straightforward, you just need to follow a few very simple steps.

First of all, you should **connect your Wallet** to Objkt and sign up.

To do this, just go to objkt.com and click "sync" on the upper right side. After that, a window like this should appear:

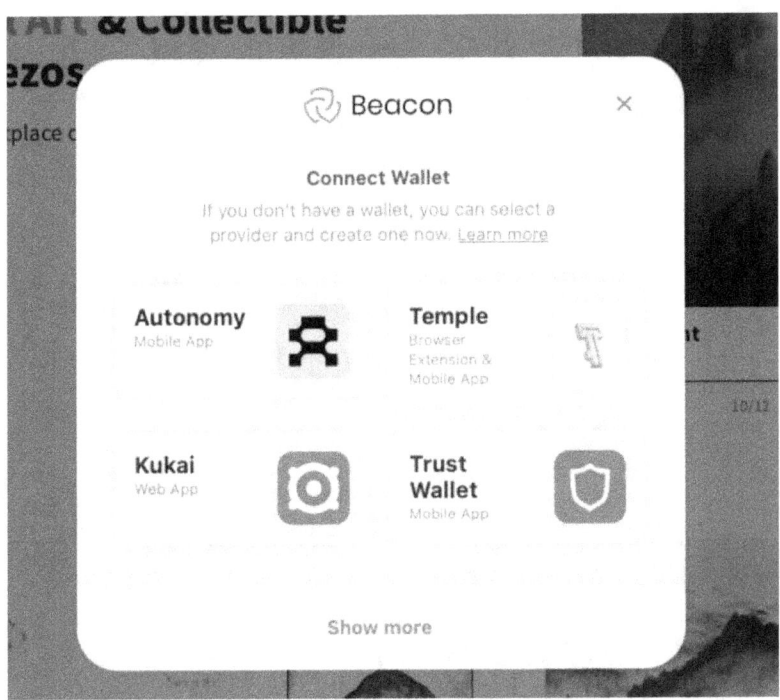

This is simply asking you to select your Tezos wallet. In our example, you would pick "**Kukai**".

After you click on Kukai, the new wallet web page will be opened. At that point, you just have to accept the connection between the wallet and Objkt, by authorising it to access your wallet's funds and NFTs.

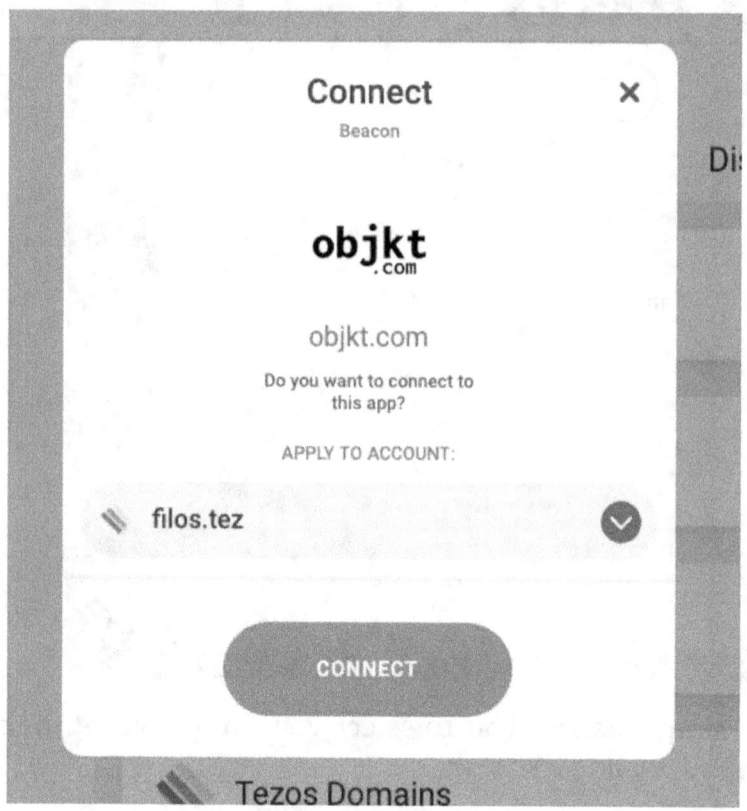

You must be **logged in** to your wallet, following the steps described in the previous paragraph.

At this point, you are **ready to mint** your first artwork on Tezos!

Add your artwork

The first step is clicking on the "Create" button that you find after clicking on your profile picture.

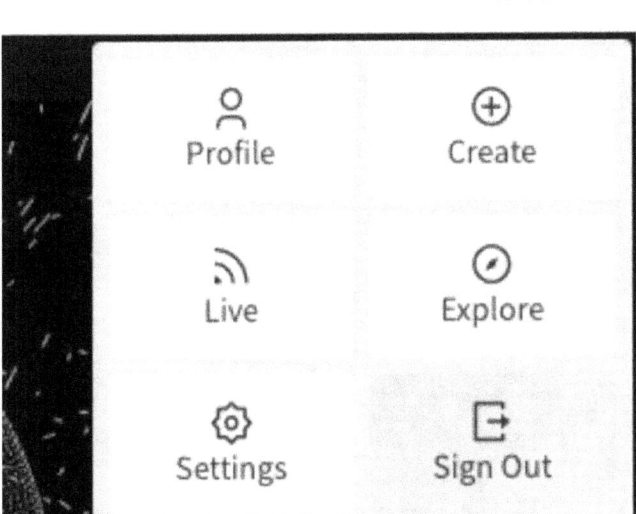

It will bring you to the following screen.

What you need to do now is just filling the different fields one by one. Let's see them closer.

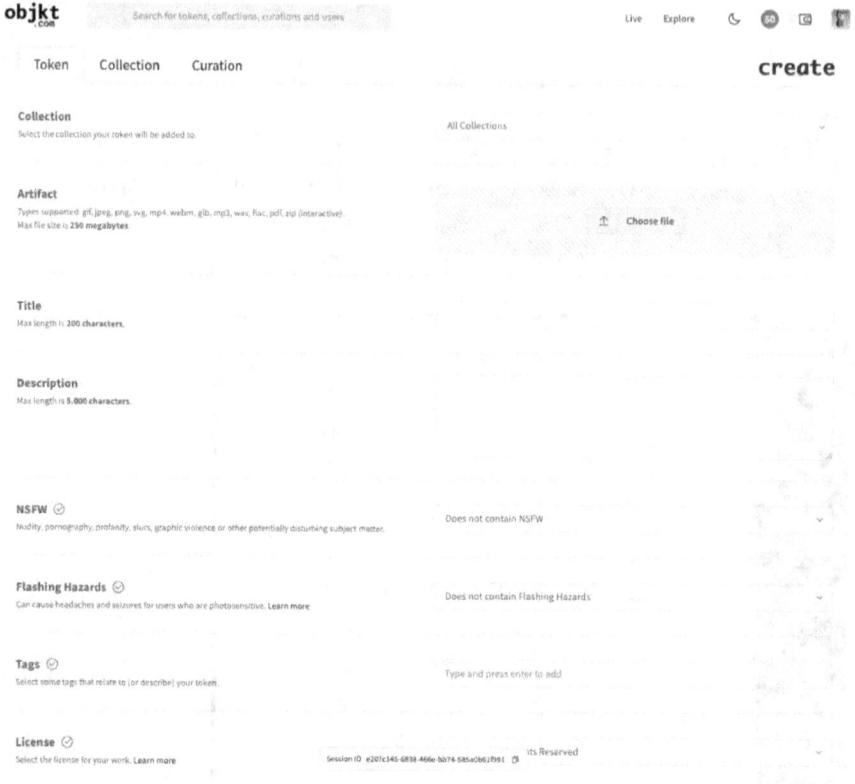

Collection

Is your artwork part of a larger collection? If you had created the collection before, then pick it from the dropdown menu, otherwise you must create a new one.

In case you have to create a new one, then just click on the "New Collection" button that will bring you to the "New Collection" tab. Here is how you can fill it.

Creating a new collection is very easy, you just need to fill the page with the following fields:

- **Logo:** upload an image that represents your collection

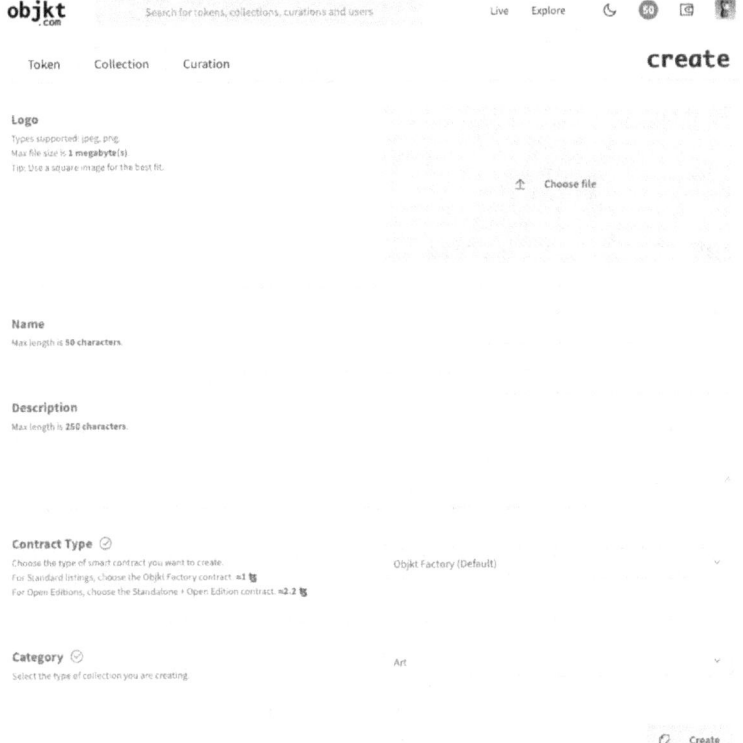

- **Name:** the name of your new collection
- **Description:** the description of your collection. Unlike the artwork, the description in this case could be shorter and straight to the point.
- **Contract type:** you should pick the standard one unless you are interested in making an open edition.
- **Category:** could be "Art" or "Collectible". Usually collectible refers to a series of similar artworks people gather, accumulate, or hoard because of their perceived value, rarity, aesthetic appeal, or personal interest, like cards, profile pictures and so on.

After you click the button "Create" on the bottom right, you have to confirm a small transaction in your wallet. It's usually around 1 Tez ($XTZ). Then your collection is ready to be filled by your beautiful artworks.

Artifact - Choose file
Your artwork must be uploaded to the platform. Just click on the button or drag & drop your file.

Title
It's the main title of your artwork. Make sure to make it unique and catchy. It's the name you will use to promote it later, too.

Description
This is VERY important. Make sure the description clearly tells the potential buyer what you had in mind when you created that artwork, what was the process behind it, and what you see in the artwork that probably others don't see. I noticed many collectors pay a lot of attention to the description. I myself sometimes buy an artwork triggered by the description of it. Make it long enough to contain all those details.

NSFW
Does your artwork contain something that may disturb someone else? Nudity? Violence? That's where you declare that.

Flashing Hazards
Certain animations may disturb someone and cause headaches and seizures for users who are photosensitive. Switch this on if that's the case.

Tags:
This is part of the metadata of your artwork. Any keyword that is a good fit with your artwork, must be listed here.

License
What is the owner of your artwork allowed to do with it? Most artists pick "All rights reserved", but there are more options.

✓ No License / All Rights Reserved
CC0 (Public Domain)
CC-BY
CC BY-SA

Attributes

This is useful in case you are publishing a series of collectibles that have specific attributes. No needed for a 1/1 or editions.

Editions

Is your artwork a 1/1, an exclusive piece of art that only one collector can own? Or you prefer to have multiple copies available? Multiple editions are quite common on Tezos, artists can make the cost cheaper for the buyer and more likely to be collected. Collectors, on the other hand, like that and do not necessarily look for a 1/1. I'm one of those, for example. This is the field you must fill with "1" (it means your artwork is a 1/1) or the number of editions you want to make available. I'll cover this topic more extensively in the next chapter.

Royalties

This represents the amount of money you want to earn each time someone else, who previously bought your artwork, sells it on the secondary market. 10% could be a good choice, but this is completely up to you.

Server

Pick Europe, America, or Asia depending on your location.

Time to Mint!

The time has come, now that you completed the steps above, you are ready to click the "Continue" button.

After you click it, a few operations will be performed and the progress will be shown in a popup window.

Then you just have to click on the "**MINT**" button (yes, finally!).

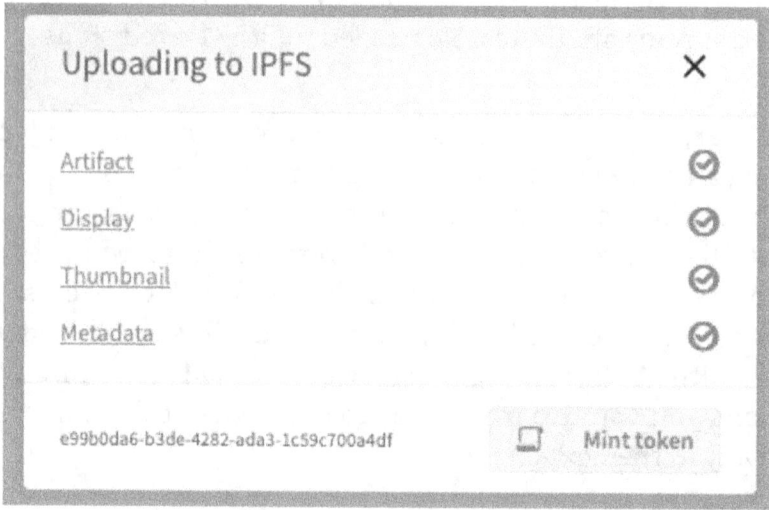

Minting an NFT requires you to pay a small fee. If you come from the Ethereum blockchain, you may notice the total cost is way cheaper. In the example shown below, the cost is around 0.089 $XTZ, equivalent to 8 USD cents at the time of writing.

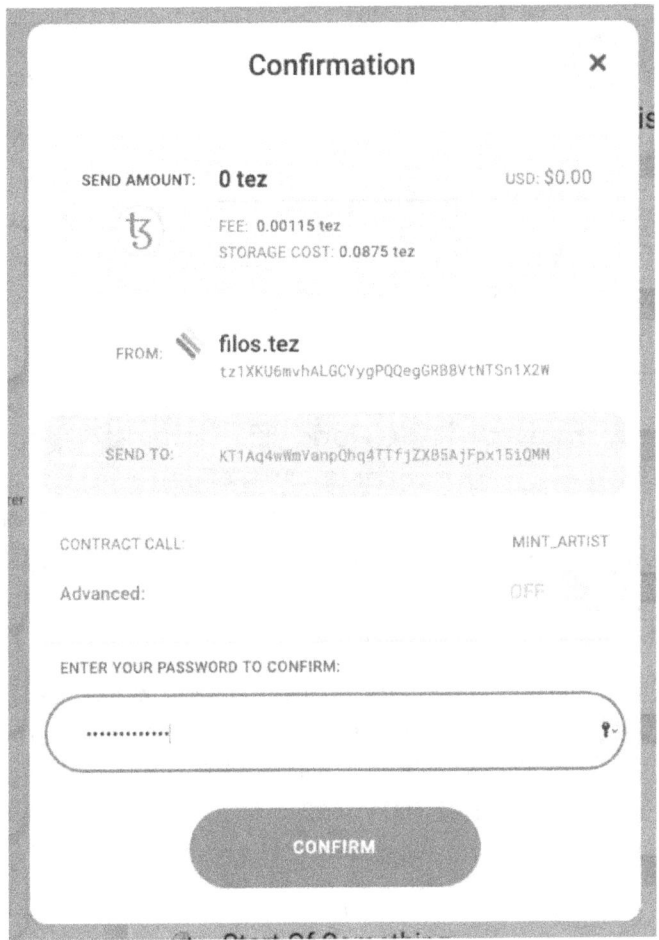

After you confirm, the mint will be completed and your artwork will now live forever on the Tezos blockchain, ready for collectors to purchase!

Objkt marketplace may take some time to show your new artwork in the "Created" section of your profile. In my experience, a few minutes. Just refresh the page until you see it.

For your reference, and if you would like to experiment, there are a few other popular marketplaces available on Tezos.

Here are some of them.

Teia: Teia is an open-source, experimental dApp is developed and maintained by the Teia Community and powered by the Tezos blockchain.

http://teia.art

Kalamint: Kalamint is another prominent NFT marketplace on Tezos that focuses on digital art and collectibles. It offers a platform for artists and creators to mint and sell their NFTs.

http://kalamint.io

FXHash: a very flexible and free marketplace on Tezos where anyone can easily mint their artwork. The interesting thing about this marketplace is that artists can generate brand new artworks by writing some lines of code that will be interpreted by the browser, giving birth to a brand new artwork each time ("generative art").

http://fxhash.xyz

Versum: Versum separates itself from the competition as a unique Tezos NFT marketplace. Versum's primary focus is on the art, user experience, and scalability. First and foremost, Versum prioritizes art. Their minimalistic UI was designed so that your eyes are drawn to the art — the platform is there, but you don't see it.

http://versum.xyz

ByteBlock: a Tezos NFT marketplace specialised in Indian and Asian market in particular.

http://byteblock.art

7. CRAFTING EDITIONS: THE ART OF SELLING LIMITED NFTS

I n the dynamic world of NFTs, the concept of scarcity takes center stage. Editions, which represent limited copies of digital artworks or collectibles, offer a captivating blend of exclusivity and accessibility. In this chapter, we'll explore the art of selling editions as NFTs, uncovering the strategies, considerations, and creative potential that accompany this unique approach.

Editions are NFTs that exist in restricted quantities, offering collectors the chance to own a piece of art with a defined scarcity factor. The allure of exclusivity drives demand. A 10 editions artwork is way more attractive than a 500 edition one.

Artists can choose the size of their editions, striking a balance between maintaining scarcity and making their work accessible to a broader audience. This decision impacts the perceived value of each NFT.

Collectors are usually drawn to limited editions as they offer a sense of rarity and uniqueness, yet they are attainable for a wider range of enthusiasts compared to 1/1 NFTs. Take also into consideration that on Tezos, selling editions is way more common than on Ethereum. On Tezos you'll find editions made of hundreds of items and collectors are happy to get one without thinking twice. On Ethereum, usually, exclusivity is a key factor and collectors might be more attracted by 1/1s.

Speaking about the price, determining the pricing of editioned NFTs is a multifaceted task. Factors include the size of the edition, the artist's reputation, and the demand within the NFT market. Auctions and reserve pricing are common methods, it's up to you.

It's also important to take into account that artists must ensure the authenticity of each edition. This often involves embedding metadata within the NFT to confirm its origin and ownership.

Whether editions or 1/1s, artists can share the story behind their work, their creative process, and inspirations to engage collectors and deepen the connection between the art and its owner. This is incredibly important and, as a collector, I always look for a story behind the artwork I'm purchasing. Make sure not to underestimate this point.

Some artists also explore fractional ownership models, where multiple collectors share ownership of a limited edition. Collaboration among artists for joint edition releases is also a growing trend, I myself own quite a few artworks result of the collaboration with multiple artists.

Artists may also offer utility to edition owners, such as access to exclusive content, events, or physical merchandise, enhancing the value proposition of owning an editioned NFT. Consider it as a "ticket" to do something or to get some perks. It's all about the type of marketing you would like to build around your work.

Editioned NFTs represent a bridge between traditional art and the digital future. They allow artists to extend their creative legacy into the blockchain era, reaching a global audience.Selling editioned NFTs is also a testament to the blend of artistry and blockchain technology. It embodies the ethos of the NFT space, where digital scarcity meets creative expression, offering artists and collectors a canvas to craft a vibrant and ever-evolving landscape of possibilities.

Now that you have all the elements needed to decide whether your first work is going to be a 1/1 or made of multiple digital copies available for collectors, let's see how you can actually sell it on Objkt.

8. SELLING YOUR ARTWORK

Now that your artwork is available on the Tezos blockchain and on the Objkt marketplace, you are ready to sell it.

Before putting it for sale, you need to pay attention to some important recommendations.

Setting the right price for your NFT artwork is crucial to attracting buyers and maximising your earnings as an artist. To determine the right price, you should consider factors such as market research, artistic value, scarcity, your reputation, costs, platform fees, and your specific goals, while remaining open to feedback and experimentation.

1. Market Research: Start by researching similar artworks and artists in the NFT marketplace. Look for pieces that are similar in style, quality, and popularity. Pay attention to the prices they have sold for or are currently listed at. This will give you a sense of the price range for your work.

2. Consider Your Reputation: Your reputation as an artist in real life can influence the price you can command. If you have an established following and a history of successful sales, you may be able to price your artwork higher than if you are just starting out.

3. Artistic Value: Assess the artistic value of your work. Consider factors such as the complexity, skill, originality, and emotional impact of your art. High-quality and unique pieces often justify higher prices. On the other hand, consider that what collectors like and love can be very different from each other.

4. Scarcity: Limited editions or scarcity can drive up the value of your NFTs (as we have seen in the previous chapter). You can create a sense of scarcity by offering only a few editions of a particular artwork or by creating exclusive variations or perks for early buyers.

5. Costs and Effort: Take into account the costs associated with creating your artwork, including materials, time, and any collaboration fees (e.g., if you hired a model or used specialized equipment)—factor in your effort and investment when determining your pricing.

6. Consider Your Goals: Consider your short-term and long-term goals. Are you looking to make a quick sale, build a collector base, or establish yourself as a high-value artist? Your pricing strategy should align with your goals.

7. Platform Fees: you usually should keep in mind the fees associated with the NFT marketplace/blockchain you choose, but in this case, as I showed you in the previous paragraph, on Tezos fees are almost zero, so this won't impact your final price.

8. Testing the Waters: If you're unsure about the right price, consider starting with a lower price for your initial NFTs to attract buyers and gain visibility. As you gain experience and gather data, you can adjust your prices accordingly.

9. Consult with Experts: If you have access to art professionals, galleries, or mentors, seek their advice on pricing. They can provide valuable insights based on their experience in the art market.

10. Feedback and Iteration: Be open to feedback from your audience and buyers. If you find that your NFTs are not selling as expected, consider adjusting your pricing strategy.

11. Promotion and Marketing: (we'll cover this in the next paragraph) Effective marketing and promotion can justify higher prices for your artwork. If you can create a strong narrative, build anticipation, and engage with your audience, buyers may be willing to pay more for the story behind the art.

Remember that pricing can be fluid in the NFT market, and it's okay to experiment and adjust your prices based on market dynamics and your evolving reputation. It's also essential to be transparent about your pricing and provide context for potential buyers, explaining the value and uniqueness of your artwork.

The price of your artwork should also depend on the number of editions you minted. Usually, the more the editions, the lower the price.

Are you ready?

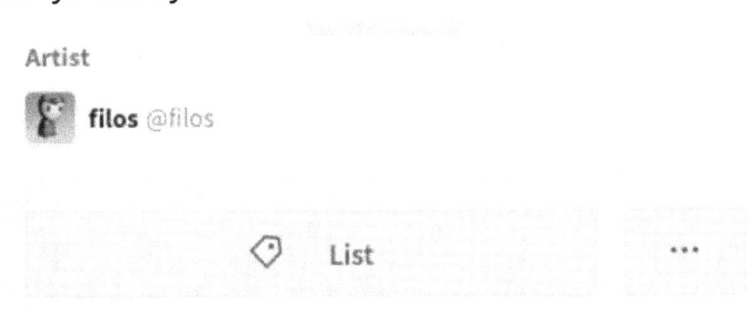

Then go to your artwork and select "LIST" button at the bottom right.

A new window appears, where you have to fill a few fields.

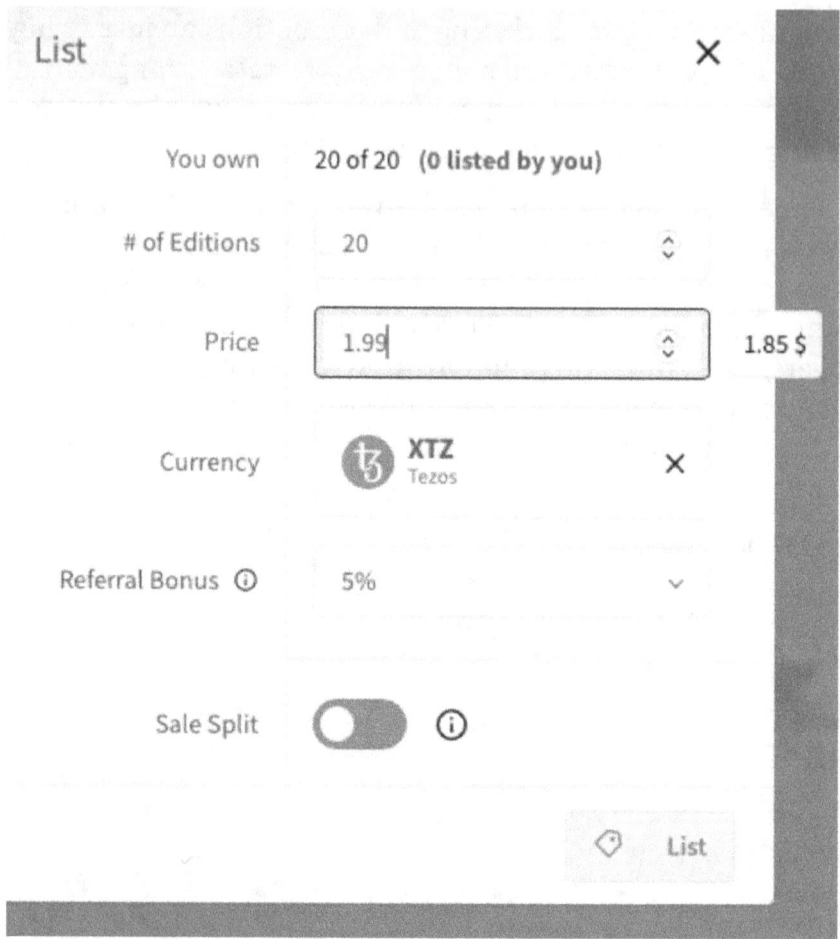

In the example above, there are 20 editions available for sale and you must put the price in the "Price" field and the number of editions in the "Editions" field. You can also set a referral bonus for those who will promote your artwork within their network.

After you click the "List" button, you will have to complete a transaction on your wallet. Again, a very small fee.

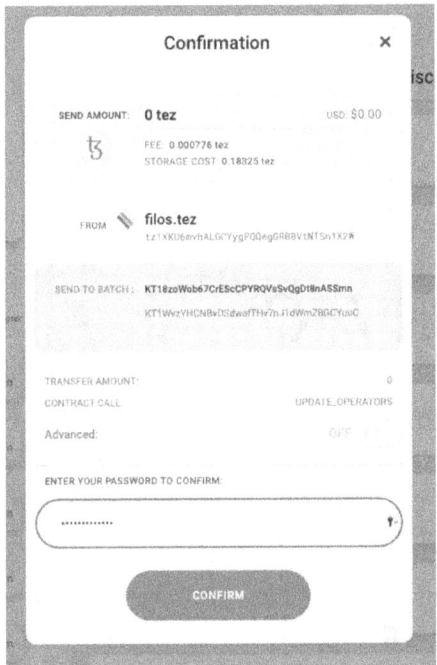

Congratulations, now you have to wait for the first buyer!

9. PROMOTING YOUR ART

Promoting and selling NFT artwork as an artist can be a rewarding endeavor, but it requires a strategic approach to gain visibility in the competitive NFT market. Here are some tips to help you get started:

1. Create High-Quality Artwork: Your art should be the focal point. Ensure that your NFT artwork is of the highest quality possible. This will attract potential buyers who value craftsmanship and creativity. Also, describing the process behind its creation is often appreciated by collectors (I love it, personally).

2. Build an Online Presence: Establish a strong online presence by creating a website or portfolio to showcase your work. Use social media platforms like X, Instagram, and TikTok to connect with your audience and share your creative process. X (formerly Twitter) is definitely the place to be, it should be your #1 priority.

3. Engage with the NFT Community: Join NFT-related forums, Discord channels, and social media groups to connect with fellow artists and collectors. Engage in discussions, collaborate on projects, and learn from others in the NFT space. This is VERY important, probably one of the most important activities you should dedicate your time to.

4. Tell Your Story: Share the story behind your artwork. Many collectors are interested in the artist's journey, inspiration, and creative process. Share insights, anecdotes, and personal experiences that make your art unique. For example, shot a video while you are creating your artwork, step by step, and share it on social media. Many collectors love that!

5. Build a Following: Cultivate a dedicated fan base by consistently sharing your work and engaging with your audience. Respond to comments, participate in discussions, and collaborate with other artists to expand your reach. Be kind, and you'll be rewarded.

6. Promote Your Listing: Actively promote your NFT listings on social media, art forums, and artist communities. Use eye-catching visuals, GIFs, or videos to showcase your NFTs. Consider running giveaways or contests to generate buzz.

7. Leverage Influencers: Collaborate with influencers in the NFT space who align with your style and vision. They can help introduce your work to a broader audience. Important: usually the real influencers are not those who present themselves as influencers.

8. Participate in NFT Drops and Auctions: Consider participating in group drops, auctions, or collaborations with other artists. These events can generate excitement and attract potential buyers.

9. Offer Perks to Collectors: Consider offering perks or incentives to early collectors, such as exclusive content, physical merchandise, or future discounts on your artwork. As discussed in the previous paragraphs, an early discounted price could make a difference.

10. Stay Informed: Stay up to date with trends, news, and developments in the NFT space. Adapt your strategy as the market evolves.

11. Be Patient and Persistent: Selling NFTs may take time. Be patient, persistent, and open to feedback. Building a successful NFT art career is often a gradual process.

Points 2 and 3 are particularly important. Let's focus on "X" for a while (formerly twitter.com).

X stands out as a favored platform for artists venturing into NFT sales for several compelling reasons. It offers a vast and diverse audience, encompassing art enthusiasts, collectors, and cryptocurrency aficionados. Moreover, X hosts a thriving art community where artists can establish connections with fellow creators, prospective buyers, and NFT collectors who actively seek digital art.

The platform's visual nature facilitates the seamless showcasing of artwork through images and tweets, allowing potential buyers to fully appreciate the creations. Furthermore, Twitter encourages direct engagement, enabling artists to interact directly with their audience through comments, likes, and retweets, fostering personal connections and building a loyal following.

X's effective use of hashtags and trending topics enhances discoverability, while its capacity for community building empowers artists to share their creative journeys and updates, fostering a sense of belonging among supporters. Collaboration opportunities with other artists often arise, expanding reach and exposure.

X serves as an immediate channel for artists to announce crucial details about NFT drops, auctions, or new releases. Additionally, the platform hosts a wealth of educational content, keeping artists informed about NFT trends and blockchain technology. The X NFT community is characterized by its supportive atmosphere, offering mentorship, guidance, and camaraderie.

In summary, X's far-reaching influence, active art community, visual capabilities, and direct engagement opportunities make it a go-to platform for artists entering the NFT market. Success, however, hinges on consistent engagement, authenticity, and a well-crafted social media strategy, providing artists with a rewarding channel to connect with a global audience of art enthusiasts.

Remember that the NFT market can be volatile, and success

may not come overnight. Building a brand and reputation as an NFT artist takes time and dedication. Keep refining your craft, engaging with your audience, and exploring new opportunities to showcase your creativity.

One more thing: here are five key users you must follow on X:

- @tezos
- @arthurB
- @tezoscommons
- @Breez_Blox
- @csoreff

10. THREE ARTISTS WHO ARE LEAVING THEIR MARK

L ast but not least, I'd like to highlight three remarkable artists who have harnessed the power of Tezos to redefine the way they share and sell their artworks. These amazing artists I got to know during my journey as a collector, serve as inspiring examples of how artists can thrive in this ever-evolving ecosystem, leveraging Tezos to showcase their unique talents and connect with a global audience. Let us delve into their stories, where art meets technology, and where the boundaries of creativity are pushed to the forefront.

1) Fer Sassali

For those who follow me on X, this name shouldn't be new to you, since I named him my "favorite" artist on Tezos. His art fits my taste perfectly and I already collected more than 30 artworks from him.

He started from a very young age. His grandfather used to draw and he would go to his house to learn. Taking advantage of photos that they found in newspaper magazines, they copied animals, faces, and objects. Then he continued learning on his own and although he had moments of more dedication, he never stopped. For some time now he has been passionate about representing thoughts, everyday and imaginary situations. He usually uses graphite pencils. Sometimes he combines them with other techniques and usually does some digital adjustments at the end. That's exactly the style I love.

A friend told him: it would be good for you to get into the world of NFTs. So, overcoming his prejudices and excuses, in August 2021 he started watching some videos. Then he took action and until today he hasn't stopped growing and learning.

Some background. Fer is an illustrator, teacher, and graphic designer who graduated from the University of Buenos Aires.

As a designer, he has extensive work experience. He participated in numerous private, public, commercial, and cultural projects.

For more than 4 years he was a professor of Graphic Design at the University of Buenos Aires.

As an illustrator, he seeks to represent thoughts, everyday situations, desire and their complexities. He proposes a permeable look, allowing the observer the production of singular fictions from their own reality.

Regarding the technique, he starts his works by hand, and then completes them digitally.

He participated in numerous fairs and collective and individual exhibitions.

He edited and published the book CROMÁTICOS. A project in which more than 50 illustrators and artists participated, contributing to the dissemination of Argentine illustration.

He was also selected by the Virtual Museum of Pachuca (Mexico), representing Argentine illustration with a virtual exhibition.

He participated in several copies of the book "The Best Latin American Illustrations" published by the University of Palermo.

Fer currently lives in Buenos Aires, Argentina and he actively participates in teaching this trade that he loves and from which he continues to learn every day.

In case you haven't noticed, the cover of this book is "powered" by one of his beautiful artworks.

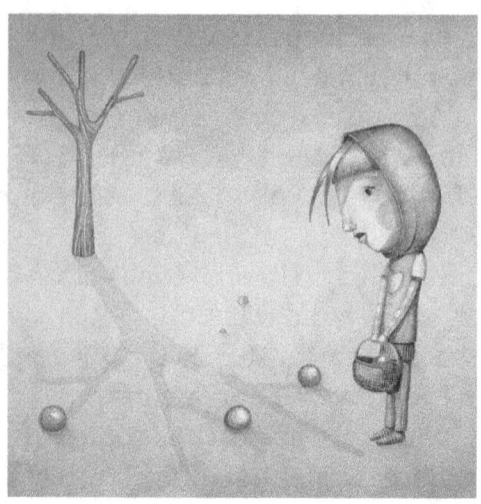

2)   Matías Roldán

This is the story of Matías Roldán, a seasoned artist, and his creative journey and entrance into the world of Web3 and Tezos.

From an early age, the creative spark was within him, an ever-present companion throughout his life. His childhood aspiration to become an artist persisted into adolescence, where a distinct internal drive pushed him forward. His artistic journey remained uninterrupted from those early years to the present, an enduring part of his life's narrative. His foray into Web3 and NFTs commenced in July 2021, spurred by a pivotal moment.

After 15 years in a demanding day job, Matías stumbled upon NFTs, driven by a need to alleviate the stress manifesting in his health. His passion for art had already taken hold, and on July 18, 2021, a mere three days after entering the space, he experienced a breakthrough moment. That day, he sold over 15 works, and within two months, the number swelled to more than 80, prompting him to leave his job behind. With over 1500 sales across different blockchain chains, his journey in the NFT realm gained remarkable momentum.

A special connection formed with the Tezos community, which he had been eager to join. The tipping point arrived in April of the following year during a meme fever when Ethereum gas fees skyrocketed. Matías recognized the opportunity and, on May 2, 2022, conducted his first drop on Objkt titled "Start Of Something."

The Tezos community welcomed him warmly, becoming his primary arena of action.

Over six months, he made more than 200 sales, cementing his presence in this vibrant community, which continues to surprise and support him.

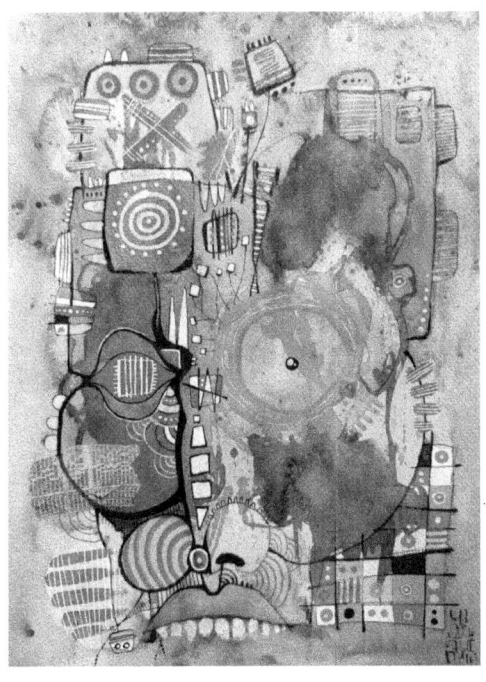

Matías Roldán, 45, hails from Buenos Aires, Argentina, a place close to his heart. Beyond his creative pursuits, he treasures his role as a partner and parent to two wonderful children. His multifaceted interests encompass astronomy, history, philosophy, chess, poetry, and music, particularly playing the bass. He dreams of one day owning a small vineyard, a testament to his love for wine.

However, his profound and unwavering passion lies in the realm of art. If he had to encapsulate his essence in one word, it would be "Poiesis," a Greek term denoting 'All Creative Process.' Matías believes that life itself is an ongoing creative journey, and each of us is a perpetual work in progress.

3) Celil Bezeng

It's funny, I still remember when I told Celil "I don't collect photography", then I started finding out that there are lots of great photographers on Tezos and many of them have a style (mostly b&w and minimalist) that I like a lot. Then I started collecting photography, too. Thanks to Celil.

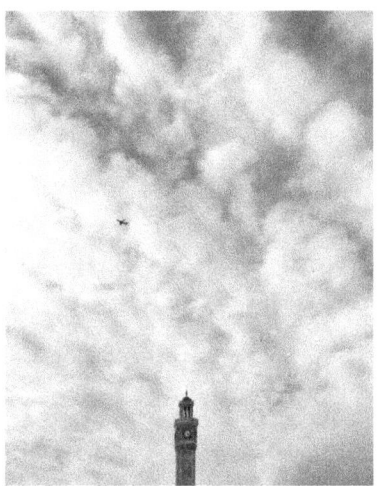

Celil has a photography and camera university education and he has been producing Analog and Digital Photography for more than 25 years. Also, 5 months ago, he discovered the great things you could do with NFTs on Tezos.

So, for the past 25 years, he has been working on analog-digital photography documents and individual works.

He also printed a Photobook and has worked as a photography instructor for many international companies, also training individual students.

I'm sure Celil will keep contributing to Tezos a lot, both as a buyer and photographer.

He currently lives in Turkey / İzmir city.

11. CONCLUSION: PIONEERING THE FUTURE OF ART ON TEZOS

I n our journey through the dynamic world of Tezos and its revolutionary impact on the art industry, we have explored the intersection of technology, creativity, and innovation. From the inception of Tezos as a blockchain network to the vibrant and thriving Tezos art marketplaces, this book has unveiled a realm of boundless possibilities for artists and art enthusiasts alike.

Tezos, with its energy-efficient, eco-friendly consensus mechanism, provides the perfect canvas for artists to unleash their creative potential. Through the creation and trading of Non-Fungible Tokens (NFTs) on Tezos-based platforms, artists are no longer confined by traditional art markets. They are free to express their visions, connect with global audiences, and gain the recognition they truly deserve.

Our exploration has also delved into the practical aspects of navigating this burgeoning ecosystem. From creating your Tezos wallet to understanding the intricacies of minting NFTs, we've equipped you with the tools to embark on your own journey of artistic exploration in the Tezos realm.

But perhaps most importantly, this book has celebrated the artists who have harnessed the potential of Tezos to not only showcase their work but also shape the future of art. We have heard the stories of those who dared to be pioneers, carving their paths in the Tezos art world, and achieving recognition and success beyond their wildest dreams.

As we conclude this journey, it's evident that Tezos is not just a technology; it's a revolution. It's an empowerment tool for artists, a platform for visionaries, and a source of inspiration for all. With the Tezos art ecosystem continuing to grow and evolve, this book serves as an invitation to seize the opportunities presented by this groundbreaking blockchain.

The canvas is yours, the colors are limitless, and the world awaits your creative journey on Tezos. Whether you are an artist, an art enthusiast, or simply curious about the future of art and blockchain technology, this book invites you to join the movement, create, promote, and appreciate art on Tezos.

Together, let us pioneer the future of art on Tezos, a world where innovation and imagination collide, forging a new artistic era unlike any other. Welcome to the Tezos Art Revolution!

ABOUT THE AUTHOR

Luca Filigheddu

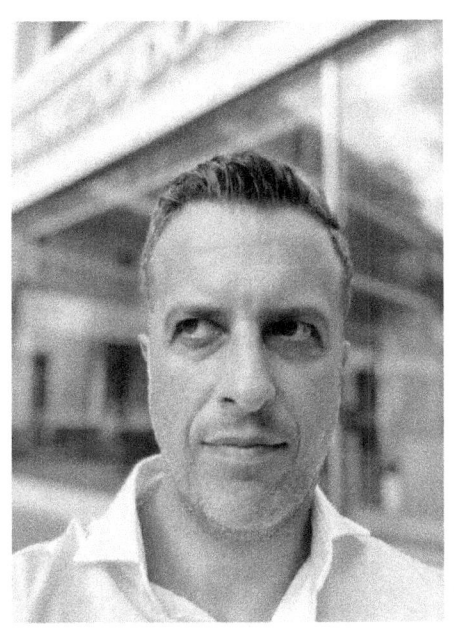

Luca Filigheddu was born in Cagliari, Italy, in 1974. Degree in Electronic Engineering, he spent most of his life in managerial roles in various startups and tech companies.

In 2021 he started investing in NFTs and just recently, in 2023, he moved his interests as a collector to the Tezos Blockchain.

Given his passionate activity investing in Tezos artists and evangelising the community about Tezos, he was awarded the Influencer Award, Formal Verification Award, Assimilation Award, and TEO Award by Tezos Commons.